My First Hebrew Word Book

pictures
by
Pépi Marzel

KAR-BEN
PUBLISHING

Note: Hebrew numbers have feminine and masculine forms. Because young children generally learn to count in the feminine form, we have used that in this book.

Text copyright © 2005 by Judye Groner and Madeline Wikler
Illustrations copyright © 2005 by Pépi Marzel

Kar-Ben Publishing, Inc.
A division of Lerner Publishing Group
241 First Avenue North
Minneapolis, MN 55401 U.S.A.
1-800-4KARBEN

Website address: www.karben.com

Library of Congress Cataloging-in-Publication Data

Groner, Judyth Saypol.
  My first Hebrew word book / by Judye Groner and Madeline Wikler ;
illustrated by Pepi Marzel.
    p. cm.
  ISBN 1-58013-126-3 (lib. bdg. : alk. paper)
 1. Picture dictionaries, Hebrew--Juvenile literature. 2. Picture dictionaries, English--Juvenile literature. 3. Hebrew language--Dictionaries, Juvenile--English. 4. English language--Dictionaries, Juvenile--Hebrew. I. Wikler, Madeline, 1943- II.
Marzel, Pepi. III. Title.
  PJ4838.G76 2005
  492.4'321--dc22
                        2004013504

Manufactured in the United States of America
1 2 3 4 5 6 – DP – 10 09 08 07 06 05

Key to Transliteration

A: as in car

E: as in bed

O: as in oh

I: as in see

U: as in boot

Ei   as in hay

Tz: as in ritz

Ch: as in Bach

אֲנִי
ani
I

שֵׂעָר
sei'ar
hair

רֹאשׁ
rosh
head

עֵינַיִם
einayim
eyes

אַף
af
nose

אָזְנַיִם
oznayim
ears

פֶּה
peh
mouth

פָּנִים
panim
face

יָדַיִם
yadayim
hands

בֶּטֶן
beten
tummy

גּוּף
guf
body

רַגְלַיִם
raglayim
legs

מִשְׁפָּחָה
mishpachah
family

חָתוּל
chatul
cat

סַבָּא
saba
grandpa

סַבְתָּא
savta
grandma

אָח
ach
brother

דּוֹד
dod
uncle

4

דּוֹדָה
dodah
aunt

תִּינוֹק
tinok
baby

אִמָּא
ima
mother

אַבָּא
aba
father

אָחוֹת
achot
sister

בְּגָדִים
b'gadim
clothes

נַעֲלַיִם
na'alayim
shoes

מִכְנָסַיִם
michnasayim
pants

סְוֶדֶר
s'veder
sweater

חוּלְצָה
chultzah
shirt

קוֹלָב
kolav
hanger

חֲצָאִית
chatza'it
skirt

כּוֹבַע
kova
hat

מְעִיל
m'eel
jacket

רְאִי
r'ee
mirror

גַּרְבַּיִם
garbayim
socks

בַּיִת
bayit
house

גַּג
gag
roof

חַלּוֹן
chalon
window

דֶּלֶת
delet
door

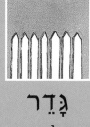

גָּדֵר
gader
fence

צִפּוֹר
tzipor
bird

דֶּשֶׁא
deshe
grass

פְּרָחִים
p'rachim
flowers

עֵץ
etz
tree

תֵּבַת דֹּאַר
tevat do'ar
mailbox

מַדְרֵגוֹת
madregot
steps

חֲדַר אוֹרְחִים
chadar orchim
living room

טֶלֶוִיזְיָה
televizya
television

סַפָּה
sapah
sofa

שָׁטִיחַ
shatiach
rug

מַחְשֵׁב
machshev
computer

טֶלֶפוֹן
telefon
telephone

שֻׁלְחָן
shulchan
table

מִטְבָּח
mitbach
kitchen

סַכִּין
sakin
knife

מַזְלֵג
mazleg
fork

כַּפִּית
capit
spoon

סִיר
siyr
pot

תַּנּוּר
tanur
oven

מְקָרֵר
m'karer
refrigerator

בֵּית סֵפֶר
beit sefer
school

תַּלְמִידִים
talmidim
students

נְיָר
n'yar
paper

מִסְפָּרַיִם
misparayim
scissors

גִּיר
gir
chalk

יַלְקוּט
yalkut
bookbag

סְפָרִים
s'farim
books

כִּסֵּא	עִפָּרוֹן	שֻׁלְחָן	צְבָעִים	לוּחַ	מוֹרָה
kisei	iparon	shulchan	tz'va'im	lu'ach	morah
chair	pencil	desk	crayons	chalkboard	teacher

מִגְרַשׁ מִשְׂחָקִים
migrash mis'chakim
playground

עֲפִיפוֹן
afifon
kite

כַּדוּר
kadur
ball

מַגְלֵשָׁה
magleshah
slide

יְלָדִים
y'ladim
children

אַרְגַּז חוֹל
argaz chol
sandbox

אוֹפַנַּיִם
ofanayim
bicycle

נַדְנֵדָה
nadnedah
swing

גַּלְגִּלִיּוֹת
galgiliyot
roller skates

חֶבֶל קְפִיצָה
chevel k'fitzah
jump rope

סַפְסָל
safsal
bench

עִיר
ir
city

אוֹטוֹבּוּס
otobus
bus

רְחוֹב
r'chov
street

מַשָׂאִית
masa'it
truck

מְכוֹנִית
m'chonit
car

מִסְעָדָה
misadah
restaurant

בִּנְיָן

binyan

building

רַמְזוֹר

ramzor

traffic light

מָטוֹס

matos

airplane

חֲנוּת

chanut

store

סִפְרִיָּה

sifriyah

library

מַכּוֹלֶת
makolet
grocery

עַגְבָנִיָּה	לֶחֶם	עוּגִיּוֹת	חָלָב	תַּפּוּחַ אֲדָמָה
agvaniyah	lechem	oogiyot	chalav	tapu'ach adamah
tomato	**bread**	**cookies**	**milk**	**potato**

עֲגָלָה
agalah
shopping cart

בֵּיצִים
beitzim
eggs

עוֹף
oaf
chicken

תַּפּוּחַ
tapu'ach
apple

תַּפּוּז
tapuz
orange

זְמַן שֵׁנָה
z'man shenah
bedtime

מִטָּה
mitah
bed

שְׂמִיכָה
s'michah
blanket

כָּרִית
karit
pillow

מְנוֹרָה
m'norah
lamp

סֵפֶר
sefer
book

שָׁעוֹן
sha'on
clock

אָרוֹן
aron
closet

דֻּבּוֹן
dubon
teddy bear

יָרֵחַ
yare'ach
moon

כּוֹכָבִים
kochavim
stars

זְמַן רַחְצָה
z'man rachtzah
bathtime

סַבּוֹן
sabon
soap

אֳנִיָּה
oniyah
boat

בּוּעוֹת
bu'ot
bubbles

אַמְבַּטְיָה
ambatya
bathtub

מַיִם
mayim
water

מַגֶּבֶת
magevet
towel

מִבְרֶשֶׁת שִׁנַּיִם
mivreshet shinayim
toothbrush

אַסְלָה
aslah
toilet

כִּיּוֹר
kiyor
sink

מִבְרֶשֶׁת שֵׂעָר
mivreshet se'ar
hairbrush

מְסִבַּת יוֹם הוּלֶדֶת
m'sibat yom huledet
birthday party

בַּלּוֹנִים
balonim
balloons

חֲבֵרִים
chaverim
friends

לֵיצָן
leitzan
clown

מַצְלֵמָה
matzlemah
camera

גְּלִידָה
g'lidah
ice cream

סוּכָּרִיָּה
sukariyah
candy

מַתָּנָה
matanah
present

נֵרוֹת
nerot
candles

עוּגָה
oogah
cake

מִיץ
mitz
juice

25

גַּן חַיּוֹת
gan chayot
ZOO

דֹּב
dov
bear

אַרְיֵה
aryeh
lion

פִּיל
piyl
elephant

נָמֵר
namer
tiger

קוֹף
kof
monkey

תּוּכִּי	נָחָשׁ	גִ'ירָפָה	גָּמָל	כֶּלֶב יָם
tuki	nachash	jirafah	gamal	kelev yam
parrot	snake	giraffe	camel	seal

אָבִיב
aviv
spring

קַיִץ
kayitz
summer

קֶשֶׁת
keshet
rainbow

גֶּשֶׁם
geshem
rain

מִטְרִיָּה
mitri'ah
umbrella

שֶׁמֶשׁ
shemesh
sun

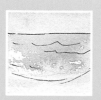
חוֹף
chof
beach

סְתָו
stav
fall

חוֹרֶף
choref
winter

רוּחַ
ru'ach
wind

עָלִים
alim
leaves

מִזְחֶלֶת
mizchelet
sled

אִישׁ שֶׁלֶג
ish sheleg
snowman

שֶׁלֶג
sheleg
snow

29

מִסְפָּרִים
misparim
numbers

אַחַת
achat
one

שְׁתַּיִם
shtayim
two

שָׁלוֹשׁ
shalosh
three

אַרְבַּע
arba
four

חָמֵשׁ
chamesh
five

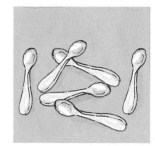

שֵׁשׁ
shesh
six

שֶׁבַע
sheva
seven

שְׁמוֹנֶה
sh'moneh
eight

תֵּשַׁע
tesha
nine

עֶשֶׂר
eser
ten

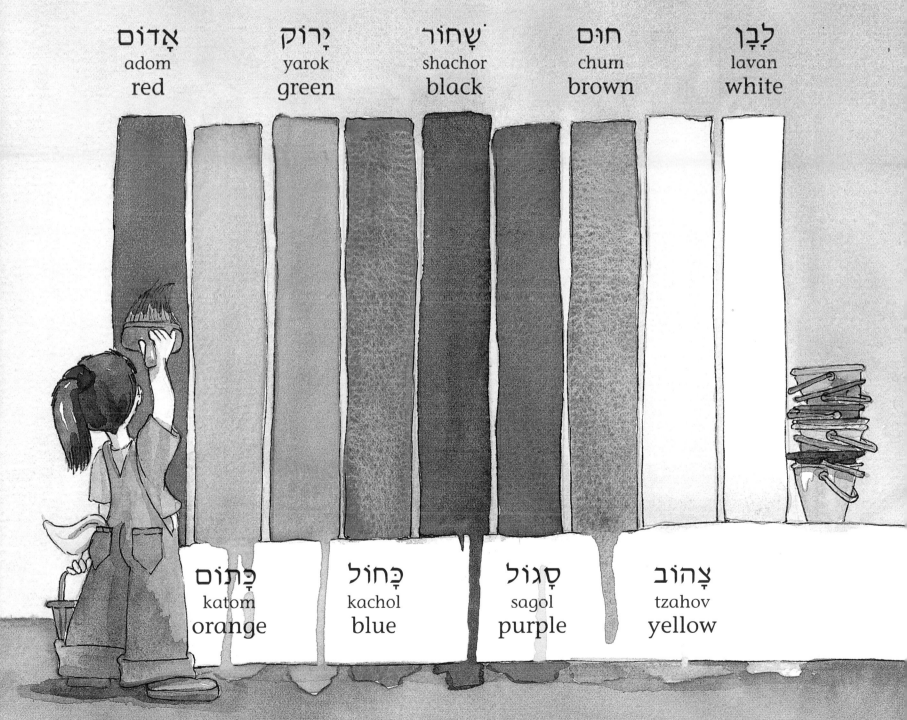

צְבָעִים
tz'va'im
colors

אָדוֹם
adom
red

יָרוֹק
yarok
green

שָׁחוֹר
shachor
black

חוּם
chum
brown

לָבָן
lavan
white

כָּתוֹם
katom
orange

כָּחוֹל
kachol
blue

סָגוֹל
sagol
purple

צָהוֹב
tzahov
yellow

Word List

English	Hebrew	Page
airplane	מָטוֹס	17
apple	תַּפּוּחַ	19
aunt	דּוֹדָה	5
baby	תִּינוֹק	5
ball	כַּדּוּר	14
balloons	בָּלוֹנִים	24
bathtime	זְמַן רַחְצָה	22
bathtub	אַמְבַּטְיָה	22
beach	חוֹף	28
bear	דֹּב	26
bed	מִטָּה	20
bedtime	זְמַן שֵׁנָה	20
bench	סַפְסָל	15
bicycle	אוֹפַנַּיִם	15
bird	צִפּוֹר	8
b'day party	מְסִבַּת יוֹם הוּלֶדֶת	24
blanket	שְׂמִיכָה	20
boat	אֳנִיָּה	22
body	גּוּף	3
book	סֵפֶר	20
bookbag	יַלְקוּט	12
books	סְפָרִים	12
bread	לֶחֶם	18
brother	אָח	4
bubbles	בּוּעוֹת	22
building	בִּנְיָן	17
bus	אוֹטוֹבּוּס	16
cake	עוּגָה	25
camel	גָּמָל	27
camera	מַצְלֵמָה	24
candles	נֵרוֹת	25
candy	סוּכָּרִיָּה	25
car	מְכוֹנִית	16
cat	חָתוּל	4
chair	כִּסֵּא	13
chalk	גִּיר	12
chalkboard	לוּחַ	13
chicken	עוֹף	19
children	יְלָדִים	14
city	עִיר	16
clock	שָׁעוֹן	21
closet	אָרוֹן	21
clothes	בְּגָדִים	6
clown	לֵיצָן	24
computer	מַחְשֵׁב	10
cookies	עוּגִיּוֹת	18
crayons	צְבָעִים	13
desk	שֻׁלְחָן	13
door	דֶּלֶת	8
ears	אָזְנַיִם	3
eggs	בֵּיצִים	19
elephant	פִּיל	26
eyes	עֵינַיִם	3
face	פָּנִים	3
fall	סְתָו	29
family	מִשְׁפָּחָה	4
father	אַבָּא	5
fence	גָּדֵר	8
flowers	פְּרָחִים	9
fork	מַזְלֵג	11
friends	חֲבֵרִים	24
giraffe	גִ׳ירָפָה	27
grandma	סָבְתָּא	4
grandpa	סָבָּא	4
grass	דֶּשֶׁא	9
grocery	מַכּוֹלֶת	18
hair	שֵׂעָר	3
hairbrush	מִבְרֶשֶׁת שֵׂעָר	23
hands	יָדַיִם	3
hanger	קוֹלָב	6
hat	כּוֹבַע	7
head	רֹאשׁ	3
house	בַּיִת	8
I	אֲנִי	3
ice cream	גְּלִידָה	24
jacket	מְעִיל	7
juice	מִיץ	25
jump rope	חֶבֶל קְפִיצָה	15
kitchen	מִטְבָּח	11
kite	עֲפִיפוֹן	14
knife	סַכִּין	11
lamp	מְנוֹרָה	20
leaves	עָלִים	29
legs	רַגְלַיִם	3
library	סִפְרִיָּה	17
lion	אַרְיֵה	26
living room	חֲדַר אוֹרְחִים	10
mailbox	תֵּבַת דֹּאַר	9
milk	חָלָב	18
mirror	רְאִי	7
monkey	קוֹף	26
moon	יָרֵחַ	21
mother	אִמָּא	5
mouth	פֶּה	3
nose	אַף	3
orange	תַּפּוּז	19
oven	תַּנּוּר	11
pants	מִכְנָסַיִם	6
paper	נְיָר	12
parrot	תּוּכִּי	27
pencil	עִפָּרוֹן	13
pillow	כָּרִית	20
playground	מִגְרַשׁ מִשְׂחָקִים	14
pot	סִיר	11
potato	תַּפּוּחַ אֲדָמָה	18
present	מַתָּנָה	25
rain	גֶּשֶׁם	28
rainbow	קֶשֶׁת	28
refrigerator	מְקָרֵר	11
restaurant	מִסְעָדָה	16
roller skates	גַּלְגִּלִיּוֹת	15
roof	גַּג	8
rug	שָׁטִיחַ	10
sandbox	אַרְגַּז חוֹל	14
school	בֵּית סֵפֶר	12
scissors	מִסְפָּרַיִם	12
seal	כֶּלֶב יָם	27
shirt	חוּלְצָה	6
shoes	נַעֲלַיִם	6
shopping cart	עֲגָלָה	19
sink	כִּיּוֹר	23
sister	אָחוֹת	5
skirt	חֲצָאִית	7
sled	מִזְחֶלֶת	29
slide	מַגְלֵשָׁה	14
snake	נָחָשׁ	27
snow	שֶׁלֶג	29
snowman	אִישׁ שֶׁלֶג	29
soap	סַבּוֹן	22
socks	גַּרְבַּיִם	7
sofa	סַפָּה	10
spoon	כַּפִּית	11
spring	אָבִיב	28
stars	כּוֹכָבִים	21
steps	מַדְרֵגוֹת	9
store	חֲנוּת	17
street	רְחוֹב	16
students	תַּלְמִידִים	12
summer	קַיִץ	28
sun	שֶׁמֶשׁ	28
sweater	סְוֶדֶר	6
swing	נַדְנֵדָה	15
table	שֻׁלְחָן	10
teacher (f.)	מוֹרָה	13
teddy bear	דֻּבּוֹן	21
telephone	טֶלֶפוֹן	10
television	טֶלֶוִיזְיָה	10
tiger	נָמֵר	26
toilet	אַסְלָה	23
tomato	עַגְבָנִיָּה	18
toothbrush	מִבְרֶשֶׁת שִׁנַּיִם	23
towel	מַגֶּבֶת	23
traffic light	רַמְזוֹר	17
tree	עֵץ	9
truck	מַשָּׂאִית	16
tummy	בֶּטֶן	3
umbrella	מִטְרִיָּה	28
uncle	דּוֹד	4
water	מַיִם	22
wind	רוּחַ	29
window	חַלּוֹן	8
winter	חֹרֶף	29
zoo	גַּן חַיּוֹת	26